The 9 Candles Of Hanukkah Tell The Tale

2023 Noah Press © All Rights Reserved

TALK TO US

hello@noah-press.com

AS THE SUN BEGAN TO SET ON THE FIRST DAY OF HANUKKAH, A CANDLE STOOD PROUD AND TALL IN THE EMPTY CANDELABRUM CALLED THE MENORAH. THE CANDLE'S NAME WAS SHAMASH, AND HE HAD THE MOST IMPORTANT JOB OF ALL.

SHAMASH WAS TALL AND SLIM AND SHONE BRIGHTLY WITH A CONFIDENT GLOW. HE STOOD PROUDLY IN THE CENTER, READY TO LIGHT UP THE OTHER CANDLES AS THEY COME. HIS WICK WAS TIGHTLY WOVEN, AND HIS SCENT WAS WARM VANILLA AND CINNAMON SPICE. SHAMASH WAS THE LEADER OF THE GROUP, PROVIDING GUIDANCE FOR HIS FELLOW CANDLES IN THE MENORAH. IT WAS THE DUTY OF THE SHAMASH TO LIGHT ALL THE OTHER CANDLES AS THE BEAUTIFUL STORY OF HANUKKAH WAS TOLD. SO, EACH EVENING, HE LIT THE CANDLE WICKS AND ENCOURAGED EACH OF THEM TO TELL THEIR PART OF THE STORY.

"HAPPY HANUKKAH!" SHAMASH SHOUTED JOYFULLY AS HE WAS LIT, AND BEAMING WITH JOY AS HE SPARKED THE FIRST CANDLE TO LIFE. "IT'S TIME TO CELEBRATE AGAIN!"

AS THE FIRST CANDLE BURST INTO FLAME, SHE SPARKLED WITH LIGHT AND JOY,
SHAMASH REMINDED HER OF WHAT HANUKKAH WAS ALL ABOUT.

HE SAID, "LONG, LONG AGO, IN 164 B.C., A BRAVE GROUP OF JEWISH WARRIORS CALLED THE MACCABEES VICTORIOUSLY DEFEATED THE SYRIAN GREEKS. YOU SEE, THE GREEKS HAD TAKEN OVER THE JEWISH TEMPLE AND DESTROYED IT.

SO, THE JEWS DECIDED TO FIGHT BACK AND RECLAIM THEIR PLACE OF WORSHIP. ONE OF THEIR LEADERS, A PRIEST NAMED JUDAH MACCABEE, LED AN ARMY TO FIGHT HARD AGAINST THE GREEKS, AND EVENTUALLY, THEY WON."

"AAH!" THE FIRST CANDLE EXCLAIMED AS SHE REMEMBERED THE REASON FOR HER EXISTENCE. SHE NEVER GREW TIRED OF HEARING THE STORY OF HANUKKAH.

IN HIS ENCOURAGING MANNER, SHAMASH ASKED HER TO CONTINUE THE STORY BY TALKING ABOUT THE GLORY OF THE TEMPLE AND WHAT IT LOOKED LIKE.
THIS CANDLE WAS A BIT SHORTER AND THICKER THAN SHAMASH. HOWEVER, SHE WAS A BEAUTIFUL GOLD COLOR AND SMELLED LIKE FRESH LEMONS AND GINGER. HER FLAME FLICKERED WITH EXCITEMENT AS SHE RETOLD THE STORY OF HOW THE MACCABEES RESTORED THE GLORY OF GOD'S TEMPLE.

"ON A SPECIAL DAY IN THE HEBREW CALENDAR CALLED KISLEV, SOMETHING AMAZING HAPPENED," SHE SAID. "THE MACCABEES CAME TOGETHER TO REMOVE THE DESTRUCTION OF THE GREEKS AND REDEDICATE THE TEMPLE. IT WAS A VERY SPECIAL DAY, AND ONE THAT WE STILL CELEBRATE TODAY!"

WHEN SHE FINISHED, SHAMASH FLICKERED HAPPILY. HE BEAMED BRIGHTER THAN EVER AND SAID, "VERY WELL DONE!"

ON THE NEXT DAY OF HANUKKAH, IT WAS THE SECOND CANDLE'S TURN. HE WAS THE SMALLEST OF THE GROUP, BUT HIS STORY WAS JUST AS IMPORTANT. HE WAS A DEEP RED COLOR AND SMELLED OF SWEET CHERRY BLOSSOMS.

HIS FLAME WAS GENTLE AND CALM, BUT BRIGHT ENOUGH TO HOLD EVERYONE'S ATTENTION. AS HE SPOKE ABOUT THE MIRACLE OF THE OIL, HIS FLAME GREW BIGGER AND BRIGHTER. IT WAS ALMOST AS IF HE WAS RELIVING THE MIRACLE HIMSELF!

"WHEN THE MACCABEES FIRST WENT INSIDE THE TEMPLE, THEY FOUND ONLY ONE SMALL JAR OF OIL THAT THEY COULD USE TO LIGHT THE MENORAH," HE EXPLAINED. "THEY KNEW THE OIL WOULD ONLY LAST FOR ONE DAY, BUT THEY LIT IT ANYWAY.

THEN, A MIRACLE HAPPENED! THE CANDLES CONTINUED TO BURN FOR EIGHT DAYS — THE EXACT AMOUNT OF TIME THE JEWS NEEDED TO PREPARE MORE OIL. THAT'S WHY, EVERY YEAR, THE JEWISH PEOPLE CELEBRATE HANUKKAH!"

WHEN HE FINISHED, SHAMASH SHOUTED, "AMEN!" THE FIRST CANDLE REJOICED IN THE MEMORY OF THE MIRACLE AS WELL. THEY IMAGINED WHAT IT WOULD BE LIKE TO BE THE MENORAH IN GOD'S TEMPLE. "THAT'S WHY THERE ARE NINE OF US," SHAMASH EXPLAINED. "I AM THE ONE WHO LIGHTS EACH OF YOU TO REPRESENT THE EIGHT DAYS THAT THE MIRACLE OIL LASTED!" THE TWO CANDLES SPARKED WITH JOY AND LOOKED AT EACH OTHER WITH LOVE AND GRATITUDE.

ON THE THIRD EVENING, IT WAS TIME FOR THE THIRD CANDLE TO BE LIT. SHE WAS BRIGHT BLUE AND SMELLED OF FRESH BLUEBERRIES. SHE HAD A FLAME THAT DANCED HAPPILY AS SHE RECOUNTED THE STORY OF THE LIBERATION.

"THE MACCABEES WON MANY IMPORTANT BATTLES AGAINST THE GREEKS," THE THIRD CANDLE SAID. "EVEN THOUGH THE JOURNEY WAS LONG AND DIFFICULT, THEY NEVER GAVE UP. AND IN THE END, THEY WON!"
SHAMASH AND THE OTHER TWO CANDLES CHEERED HAPPILY. THEY BEAMED AT THE THOUGHT OF THE MACCABEES' VICTORY!

BY THE FOURTH EVENING, SHAMASH PROUDLY LIT CANDLE NUMBER FOUR AND WAITED FOR HIM TO TELL HIS PART OF THE STORY. HE WAS ALSO BLUE, LIKE CANDLE NUMBER THREE, BUT A BIT LIGHTER IN COLOR.

HE SAID, "THE MACCABEES WERE OVERJOYED TO TAKE BACK CONTROL OF THEIR OWN LAND AND PRACTICE THEIR TRADITIONS AGAIN. THESE JEWISH WARRIORS WERE KNOWN FOR THEIR COURAGE AND STRENGTH. THEY SET A GOOD EXAMPLE FOR US AND REMIND US OF HOW THE JEWISH PEOPLE HAVE NEVER GIVEN UP!"

WITH THAT, THE OTHER CANDLES CHEERED. THEY WERE PROUD OF THEIR HERITAGE AND WANTED TO BE STRONG LIKE THE MACCABEES.

ON EVENING NUMBER FIVE, THE FIFTH CANDLE WAS LIT. SHE WAS A BEAUTIFUL SHADE OF GREEN AND SMELLED LIKE PINE TREES IN THE FOREST! SHE HAD A WIDE, CIRCULAR FLAME THAT LIT UP THE ROOM, AND SHE SPOKE PROUDLY ABOUT THE TRADITIONS CELEBRATED DURING HANUKKAH.

"ONE OF THE BEST THINGS ABOUT HANUKKAH ARE THE DELICIOUS FOODS THAT ARE PREPARED," SHE SAID. "TWO TRADITIONAL FOODS ARE SUFGANIYOT AND LATKES. SUFGANIYOT ARE DEEP-FRIED DONUTS THAT ARE FILLED WITH YUMMY JELLY. LATKES ARE POTATO PANCAKES THAT ARE FRIED UNTIL THEY ARE CRISPY AND GOLDEN. BOTH OF THESE TASTY TREATS ARE COOKED IN OIL TO REPRESENT THE LONG-LASTING OIL IN THE TEMPLE."

WHEN SHE FINISHED, EVERYONE SMILED. THE DELICIOUS FOODS OF HANUKKAH WERE ONE OF THEIR FAVORITE CELEBRATIONS!

AS EVENING NUMBER SIX ROLLED AROUND, SHAMASH LIT THE BRIGHT YELLOW CANDLE WITH THE WIDE BASE AND TALL FLAME THAT FLICKERED JOYFULLY. THE SIXTH CANDLE'S SCENT REMINDED THE OTHER CANDLES OF A SUNNY DAY IN PARADISE. HE HAD THE MOST CHEERFUL PERSONALITY!

THIS CANDLE REMINDED EVERYONE TO EMBRACE THE JOYOUS NATURE OF HANUKKAH AND NOT TO TAKE THE CELEBRATION FOR GRANTED.
"IT'S IMPORTANT TO HAVE FUN DURING HANUKKAH!" HE SAID. "GIVING GIFTS, SINGING SONGS, AND PLAYING DREIDEL GAMES MAKES THE HOLIDAY EXTRA SPECIAL!"

SHAMASH AND THE OTHER CANDLES SMILED IN REMEMBRANCE. THEY LOVED WATCHING FAMILIES CELEBRATE HANUKKAH TOGETHER. THEY HAD SEEN MANY GAMES OF DREIDEL BEING PLAYED WITH THE SPECIAL WOODEN PIECES THAT SPUN AROUND AND AROUND.

"WHEN OUR FLAMES START DANCING," HE SAID, "THEY FILL THE ROOM WITH WARM LIGHT AS EVERYONE GATHERS AROUND. IT IS OUR JOB TO BRING THE HOLY LIGHT DEEP INTO THEIR HEARTS." SHAMASH SMILED AND ENCOURAGED THE SEVENTH CANDLE TO SHARE MORE.

"FOR THE FIRST HALF-HOUR AFTER WE'RE LIT," CANDLE SEVEN EXPLAINED, "SOMETHING VERY SPECIAL HAPPENS. IT'S A TIME WHEN WE ALL TAKE A BREAK FROM OUR USUAL BUSY TASKS. WE CALL IT "MELACHA," AND IT MEANS THAT WE REST FROM OUR WORK."

THE OTHER CANDLES WERE QUIET AS THEY RESPECTED THE WORDS OF THE SEVENTH CANDLE. IT WAS IMPORTANT FOR THEM TO SHINE THEIR HOLY LIGHT AND ENCOURAGE A MOMENT OF REST.

AS THE FINAL EVENING OF HANUKKAH ARRIVED, IT WAS TIME FOR CANDLE NUMBER EIGHT TO SPEAK. EVERYONE GAVE HER THEIR UNDIVIDED ATTENTION. THIS CANDLE WAS A DEEP PURPLE COLOR, AND HER SCENT WAS A MIXTURE OF LAVENDER AND ROSE.

HER STORY WAS THE GRAND FINALE, AND SHE SPOKE WITH PASSIONATE ENERGY, PAINTING A VIVID PICTURE OF THE HOLINESS OF HANUKKAH.

"DURING HANUKKAH, WE ADD TWO SPECIAL PRAYERS TO OUR DAILY ROUTINE," SHE SAID. "ONE OF THESE PRAYERS IS CALLED HALLEL, WHICH IS LIKE A HAPPY SONG OF THANKSGIVING. WE SAY THIS PRAYER IN THE MORNING, AND IT HELPS US FEEL JOYFUL THROUGHOUT THE DAY.

THE OTHER SPECIAL PRAYER IS CALLED AL HANISIM. THIS PRAYER HELPS US REMEMBER ALL THE AMAZING THINGS GOD HAS DONE FOR US. THESE PRAYERS HELP US CONNECT EVEN MORE DEEPLY WITH OUR FAITH AND FEEL THE JOY AND WONDER OF HANUKKAH."

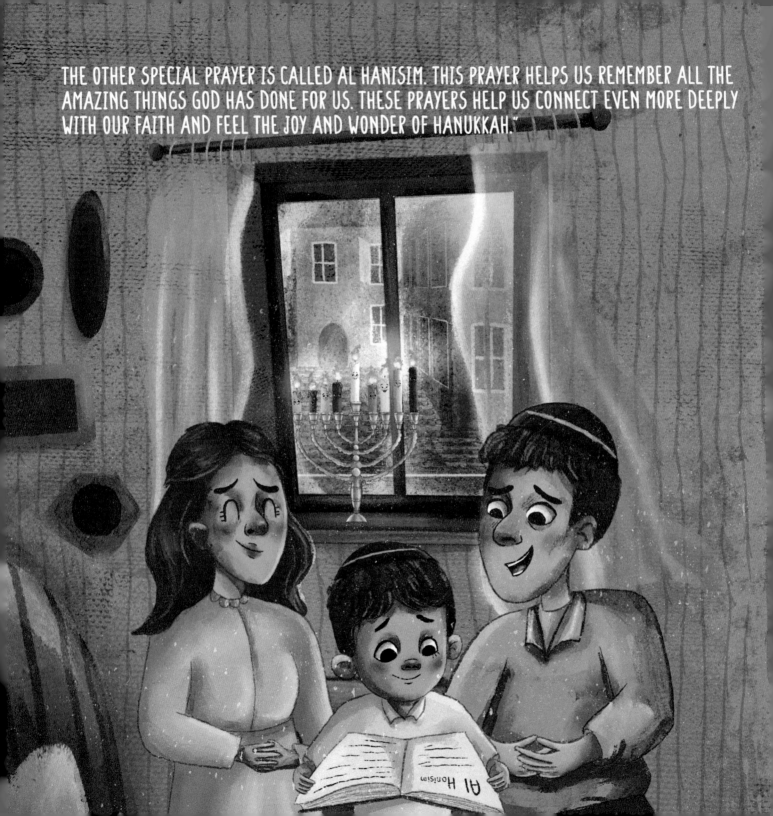

SHAMASH BEAMED WITH HAPPINESS AT THE CANDLES IN THE MENORAH. EACH OF THEM HAD DONE A MARVELOUS JOB RETELLING THEIR PART OF THE STORY. WITH THAT HAPPY ENDING, THE NINE CANDLES CONTINUED TO SHINE, AND PROMISED TO ALWAYS SHARE THE WONDERFUL STORY OF HANUKKAH.

Made in the USA
Las Vegas, NV
04 December 2023